Logo Coloring Book

Victor Langer

ISBN 9798648276352

To Raz,
the Razcal

Coloring, if properly done,
can be something more than fun.

Just do it very mindfully,
and it's a kind of therapy.

Think of it as concentration.
You could also call it meditation.

With every red you feed your head.
With every green you grow serene.

Each blue will show you something new,
and every yellow will say hello.

Yes, every tint and shade and hue
will help you be a better you,

and every colorful design
will show you how you can refine

your consciousness, for this is true:
as you color it, it colors you.

Contents

 8 House Heart Interlace

 15 Space Cube

 9 Exploded View

 16 Triple Double-Circle Interlace

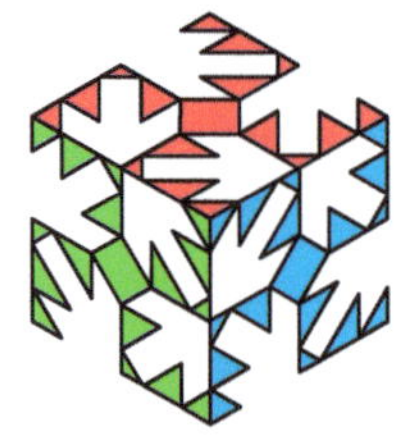 10 Twelve Arrow Cube

 17 Ten Star Interlace

 11 Five Square Interlace

 18 Four Interlaced Loops

 12 Origami Crane Ring

 19 Three Cubicle Frame Interlace

 13 Quilt Star

 20 Checker Heart

 14 Twisted Ribbon

 21 Triple Cross

 22 Three Arrow Target

 30 Caning

 23 Arrows on Sphere

 31 Nine Cube Ring

 24 Cube of Rotating Squares

 32 Dome of Triangles

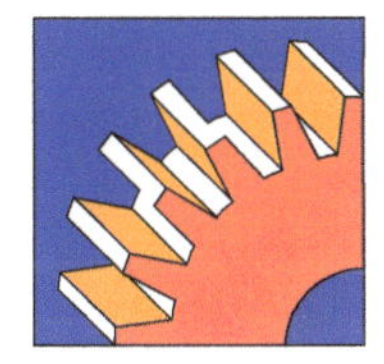 25 Gear

 33 Six Flower Wreath

 26 Four Wheel Overlap

 34 Meandering Cube

 27 Echo

 35 Pinwheel Wheel

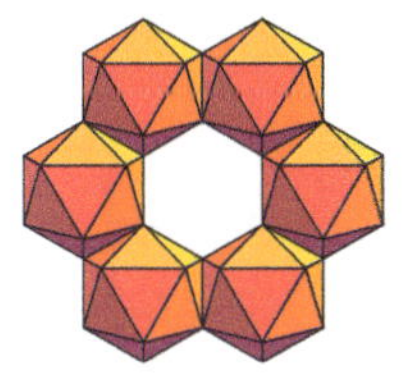 28 Six Icosahedron Ring

 36 Eight Square Overlap

 29 Hanger Tangle

 37 Wing Thing

House Heart Interlace

8

Exploded View
9

Twelve Arrow Cube

10

Five Square Interlace

11

Origami Crane Ring

12

Quilt Star

13

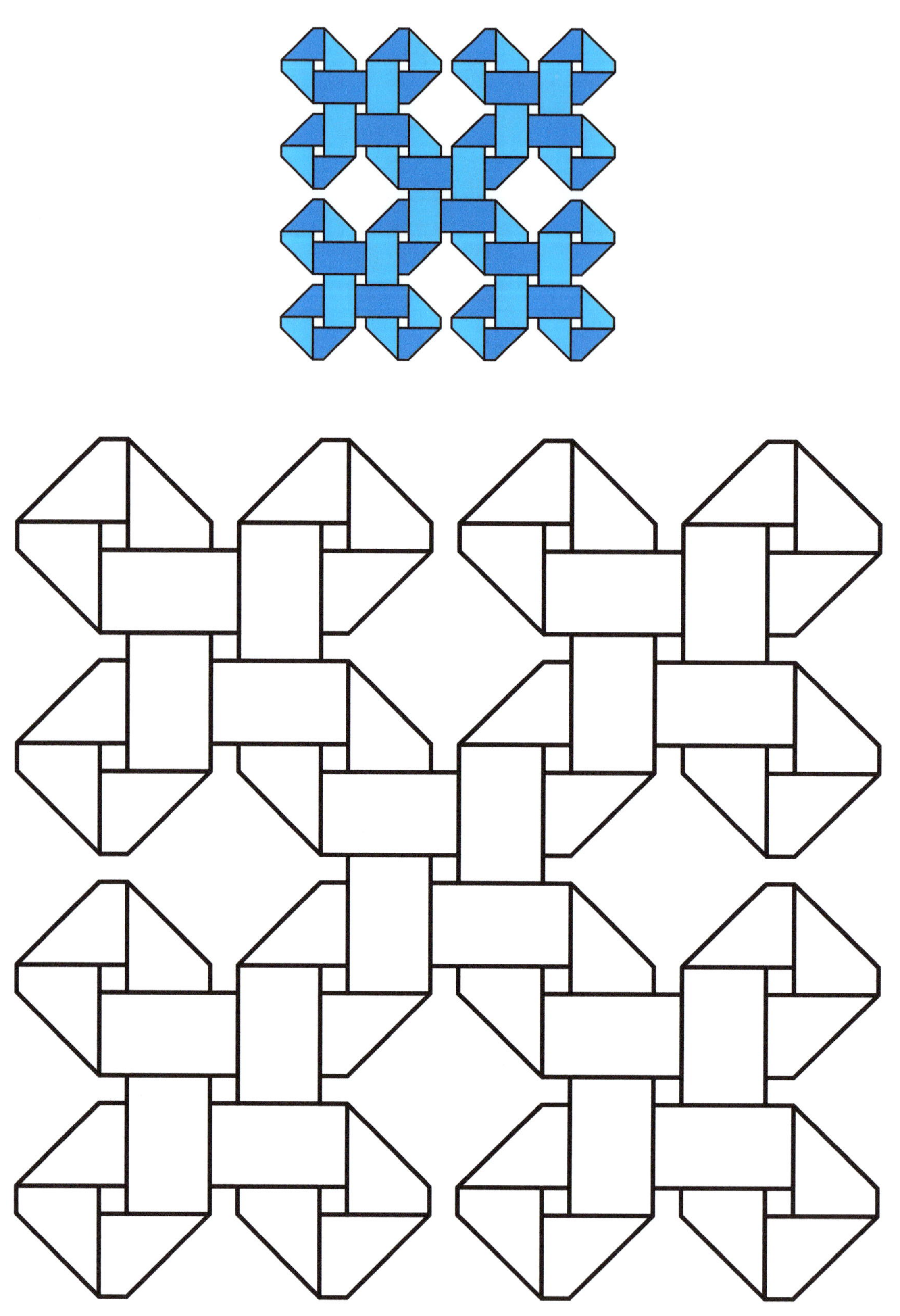

Twisted Ribbon
14

Space Cube

15

Triple Double-Circle Interlace
16

Ten Star Interlace
17

Four Interlaced Loops
18

Three Cubicle Frame Interlace
19

Checker Heart
20

Triple Cross

Three Arrow Target

22

Arrows on Sphere
23

Cube of Rotating Squares
24

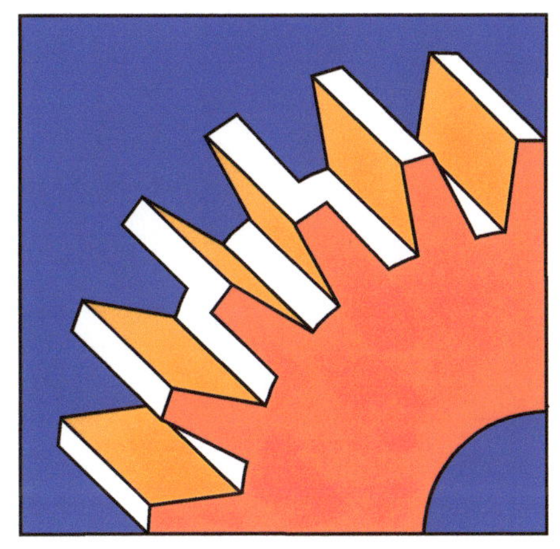

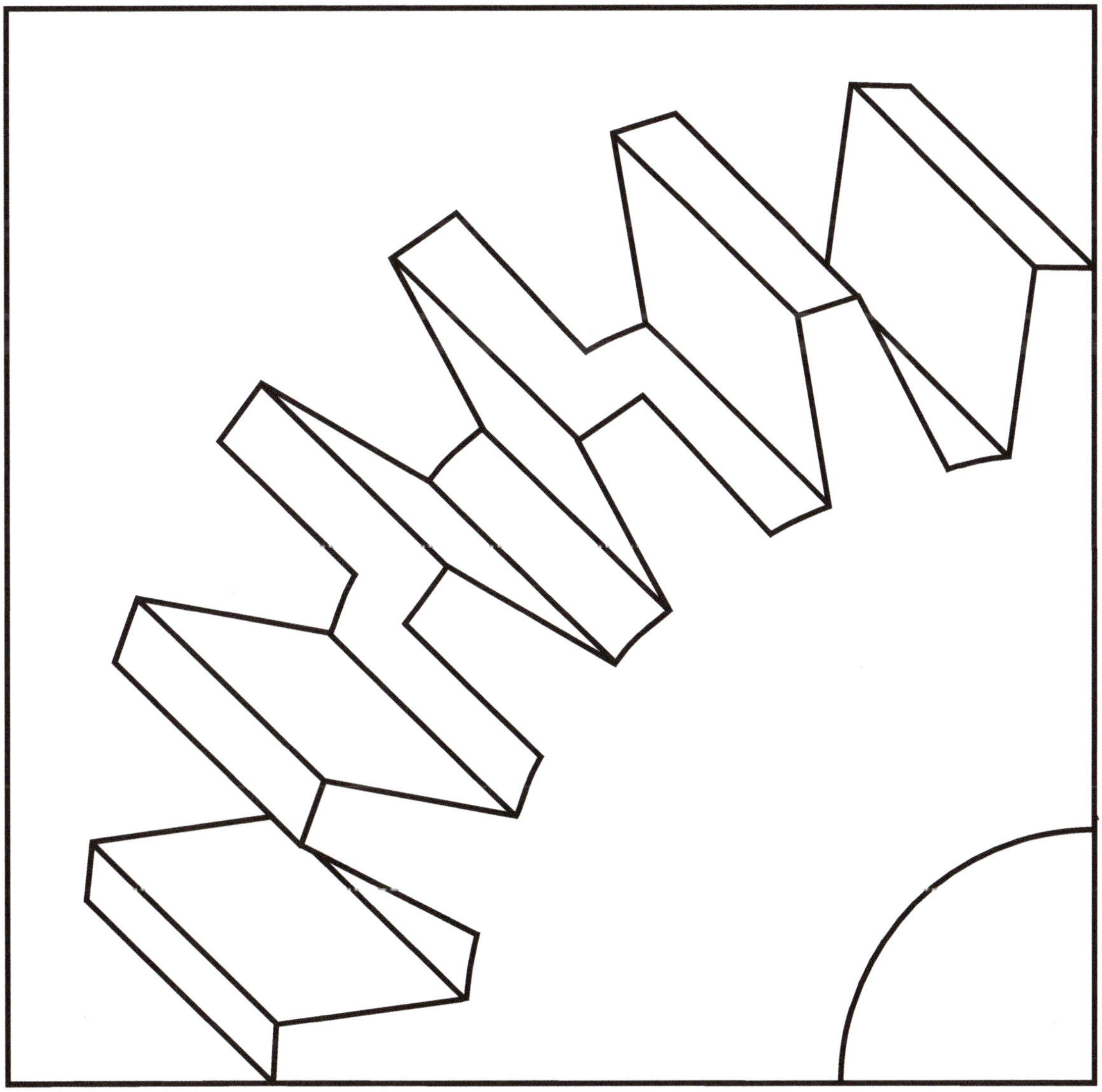

Gear
25

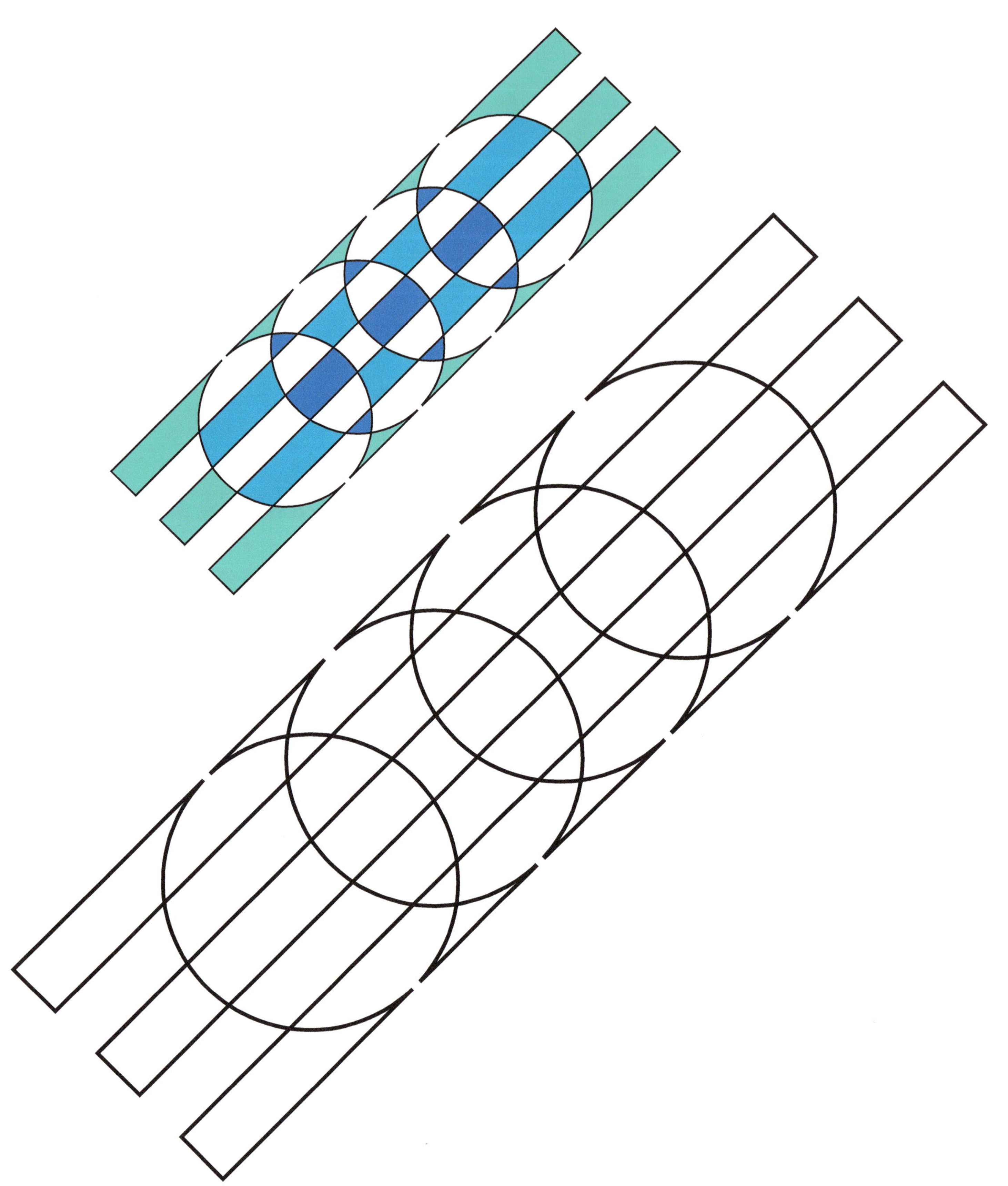

Four Wheel Overlap
26

Echo

27

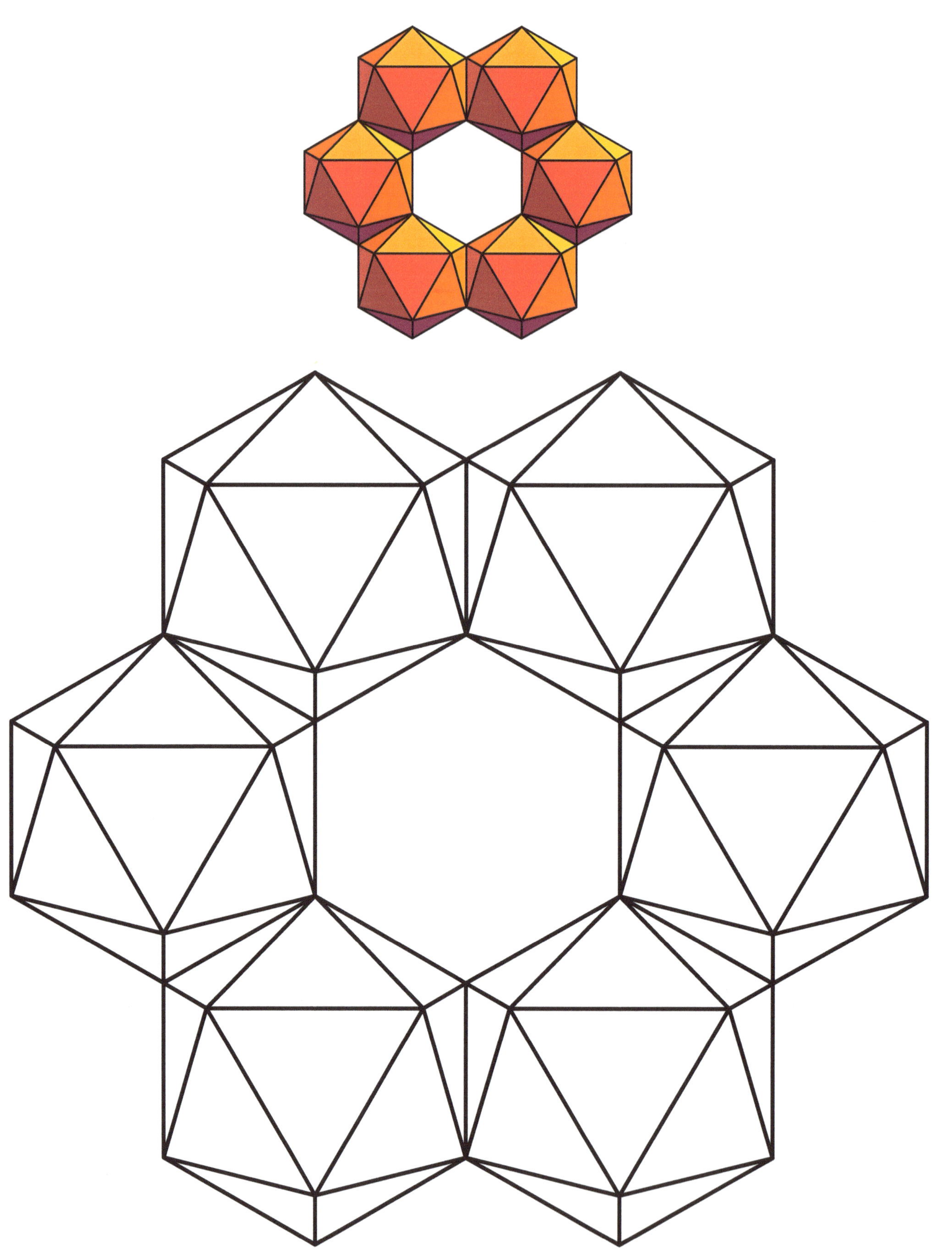

Six Icosahedron Ring
28

Hanger Tangle

29

Caning
30

Nine Cube Ring
31

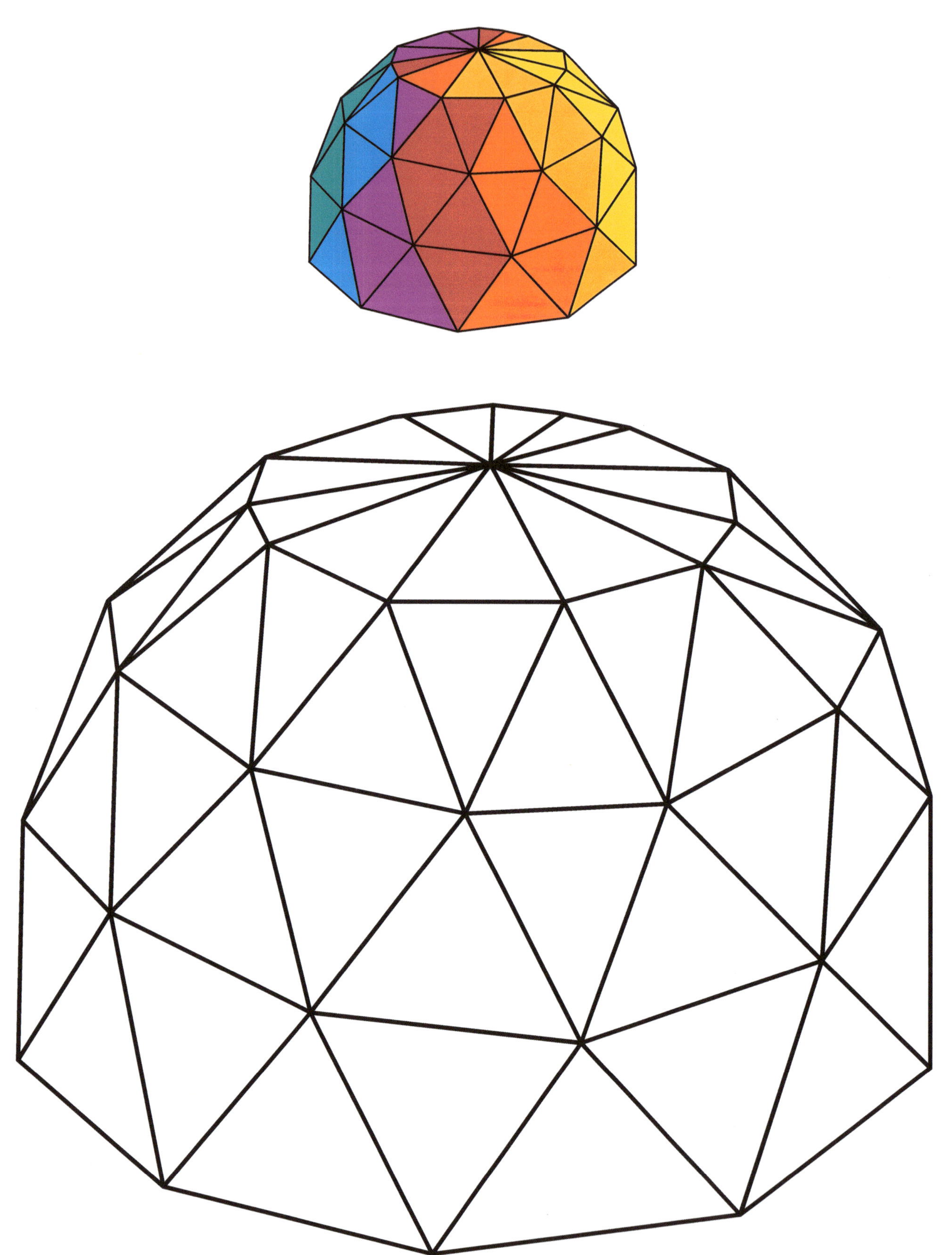

Dome of Triangles
32

Six Flower Wreath

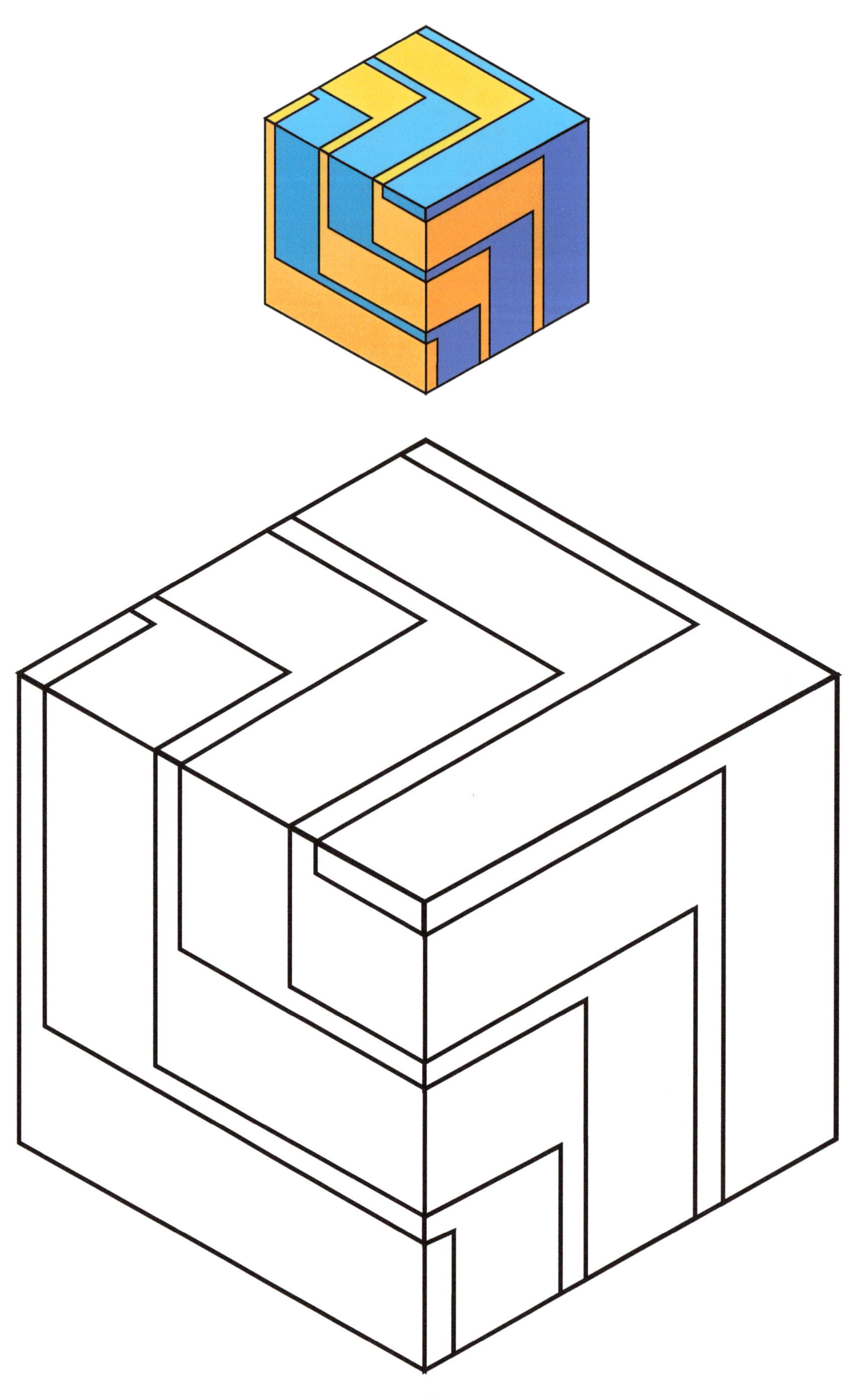

Meandering Cube

34

Pinwheel Wheel

35

Eight Square Overlap
36

Wing Thing
37

About the Author

Victor Langer is a writer and
graphic designer
in the San Francisco area.
His other books are:

Riddle Poems for ages 3 to 7
1040 for Dogs, and other tax forms
Geriacula, the Senile Vampire
The Whole Whog Catalog
The Nuclear War Fun Book
Surviving Your Baby & Child

His books have received praise in
The New York Times,
The Wall Street Journal,
The New York Daily News,
and *New York Magazine.*